GROWING CLOSER TO GOD

The Living as a Christian Series:

Basic Christian Maturity

Growing in Faith
Steve Clark
Knowing God's Will
Steve Clark
Decision to Love
Ken Wilson
God First
Ken Wilson
Sons and Daughters of God
Ken Wilson
Growing Closer to God
Tom Gryn

Overcoming Obstacles to Christian Living

How to Repair the Wrong You've Done
Ken Wilson
Getting Free
Bert Ghezzi

The Emotions

The Angry Christian
Bert Ghezzi
The Self-Image of a Christian
Mark Kinzer
Living with a Clear Conscience
Mark Kinzer

Christian Character

Strength under Control
John Keating
How to Become the Person You Were Meant to Be
Peter Williamson

Personal Relationships

Taming the Tongue
Mark Kinzer

Growing Closer to God

Tom Gryn

SERVANT BOOKS
Ann Arbor, Michigan

Published by Servant Books
P.O. Box 8617
Ann Arbor, Michigan 48107

Cover photo by H. Armstrong Roberts
Book Design by John B. Leidy

Printed in the United States of America
ISBN 0-89283-160-X

Contents

Living as a Christian

IN HUMAN TERMS, it is not easy to decide to follow Jesus Christ and to live our lives as Christians. Jesus requires that we surrender our selves to him, relinquish our aspirations for our lives, and submit our will to God. Men and women have never been able to do this easily; if we could, we wouldn't need a savior.

Once we accept the invitation and decide to follow Jesus, a new set of obstacles and problems assert themselves. We find that we are often ignorant about what God wants of us as his sons and daughters. For example, what does it mean practically to obey the first commandment—to love God with our whole mind, heart, and strength? How can we know God's will? How do we love people we don't like? How does being a Christian affect what we do with our time and money? What does it mean "to turn the other cheek?" In these areas—and many others—it is not easy to understand exactly what God wants.

Even when we do know what God wants, it can be quite difficult to apply his teaching to our daily lives. Questions abound. How do we find time to pray regularly? How do we repair a relationship with someone we have wronged or who has wronged us? How do we handle unruly emotional reactions? These are examples of perplexing questions about the application of Christian teaching to our daily lives.

Furthermore, we soon discover that Christians have enemies—the devil outside and the flesh within. Satan tempts us to sin; our inner urges welcome the temptation, and we find our will to resist steadily eroding.

Finally, we must overcome the world. We are living in an environment that is hostile toward what Christians believe and how they live, and friendly toward those who believe and do the opposite. The world in which we live works on our Christian resolve in many subtle ways. How much easier it is to think and act like those around us! How do we persevere?

There is a two-fold answer to these questions: To live successfully as Christians, we need both grace and wisdom. Both are freely available from the Lord to those who seek him.

As Christians we live by grace. The very life of God works in us as we try to understand God's teaching, apply it to our lives, and overcome the forces that would turn us aside from our chosen path. We always need grace and grace is always there. The Lord is with us always, and the supply of his grace is inexhaustible.

Yet grace works with wisdom. Christians must *learn* a great deal about how to live according to

God's will. We must study God's word in scripture, listen to Christian teaching, and reflect on our own experience and the experience of others. Many Christians today lack this kind of wisdom. This is the need which the *Living as a Christian* series is designed to meet.

The book you are reading is part of a series of books intended to help Christians apply the teaching of scripture to their lives. The authors of *Living as a Christian* books are pastoral leaders who have given this teaching in programs of Christian formation in various Christian communities. The teaching has stood the test of time. It has already helped many people grow as faithful servants of the Lord. We decided it was time to make this teaching available in book form.

All the *Living as a Christian* books seek to meet the following criteria:

- **Biblical.** The teaching is rooted in scripture. The authors and editors maintain that scripture is the word of God, and that it ought to determine what Christians believe and how they live.

- **Practical.** The purpose of the series is to offer down-to-earth advice about living as a Christian.

- **Relevant.** The teaching is aimed at the needs we encounter in our daily lives—at home, in school, on the job, in our day-to-day relationships.

- **Brief and Readable.** We have designed the series for busy people from a wide variety of backgrounds. Each of the authors presents profound Christian truths as simply and clearly as possible, and illustrates those truths by examples drawn from personal experience.

- **Integrated.** The books in the series comprise a unified curriculum on Christian living. They do not present differing views, but rather they take a consistent approach.

The format of the series makes it suitable for both individual and group use. The books in *Living as a Christian* can be used in such group settings as Sunday school classes, adult education programs, prayer groups, classes for teenagers, women's groups, and as a supplement to Bible study.

The *Living as a Christian* series is divided into several sets of books, each devoted to a different aspect of Christian living. These sets include books on Christian maturity, emotions in the Christian life, the fruit of the Holy Spirit, Christian personal relationships, Christian service, and, very likely, on other topics as well.

This book, *Growing Closer to God,* is part of a set of books which communicates essential Christian wisdom for maturing in Christ. To grow in living the Christian life, we must learn about faith, love of God, love of neighbor, and our identity as sons and daughters of God, to name just a few topics.

To reach spiritual maturity, Christians must know how God enables us to overcome the obstacles that inevitably arise: our own wrongdoing, the power of the world, the flesh, and the devil. *Growing Closer to God* and other books in this set present practical, scripturally based teaching that will help you attain basic maturity in your Christian life.

The editors dedicate the *Living as a Christian* series to Christian men and women everywhere who have counted the cost and decided to follow Jesus Christ as his disciples.

Bert Ghezzi and Peter Williamson
General Editors

Preface

THE OTHER DAY, I came across some instructions that Francis of Assisi wrote for the men who joined him in the early days of his ministry. He told them:

> We should wish for nothing else and have no other desire, we should find no pleasure or delight in anything except in our Creator, Redeemer, and Savior. . . . Nothing then, must keep us back, nothing separate us from him, nothing come between us and him. At all times and seasons, in every country and place, every day and all day we must have a true and humble faith and keep him in our hearts. . . . He is unchangeable, invisible, indescribable and ineffable, incomprehensible, unfathomable, blessed and worthy of all praise, glorious, exalted, sublime, most high, kind, lovable, delightful and utterly desirable beyond all else, forever and ever.

Francis' exhortation expressed a call to total dedication, a call that is shocking in its implications. I reread it out loud and thought about it for a while. And as I did, I experienced two contradictory feelings—first, a strong desire to serve the Lord with similar abandonment and, second, a vague fear that such total commitment was impractical, maybe even unpleasant. And yet, as I thought about the lives of men and women who had just such a relationship with God—St. Paul, John Wesley, Mother Teresa of Calcutta—I realized that their lives were characterized by a fullness and joy rarely seen elsewhere.

The central challenge of each of our lives is to grow in our relationship with God until he becomes the focus of all we do. This challenge is the most rewarding goal we can have. In fact, once we begin to live by the Spirit, we will have no choice but to walk by the Spirit, if we are to continue along the paths that will lead us closer to God. Whenever we begin to fear that this challenge will prove too much for us, we must remember the words of Paul, "I consider that the sufferings of this present time are not worth comparing with the glory that is to be revealed to us" (Rom 8:18). And when our determination begins to slip, we should return to the Spirit, asking for a renewal of the highest vision: "And we all, with unveiled face, beholding the glory of the Lord, are being changed into his likeness from one degree of glory to another; for this comes from the Lord who is the Spirit" (2 Cor 3:18). Our relationship with God is affected by our decisions, attitudes, and approaches. The purpose of this book is to discuss all these areas in an attempt to help us grow closer to God. By God's grace, may we all grow quickly into the people he wants us to be.

ONE

Loving God
The Goal of Life

SOME YEARS AGO I was invited by a friend to attend an informal prayer meeting in a neighboring city. That was the first time I ever considered travelling forty miles to gather with people in a house simply to pray. And yet I found myself saying yes to the invitation.

As we drove to the meeting, I began to imagine what it would be like, but I was surprised by what met us. We entered the house, taking our place quietly in the living room. About thirty people were present, and everyone sang a few songs and prayed together, sharing what God had been doing in their lives. I was struck by the fact that these people acted as though God was right there with them. They prayed as if they were engaging in a two-way conversation with God, and they talked about God as if they and God both knew each other very well.

As I sat there, a deep desire began to well up in me to know God in that same intimate way. I had been raised a Christian and had often prayed, either in church or by myself. But I had always thought of God as someone a bit more distant. I talked to him but never expected him to talk to me. I thought God surveyed my everyday activities from a distance, occasionally taking a closer look to be sure that all was going well. But that day I met people who had a different relationship with God, a much more personal one. They talked as though God was a father to them, as though Jesus loved them like a brother and was always with them. It was as though they were on a team with God, and he was on their side, even when it came to helping them with details of their daily lives. Right then I made a decision. I would find out how I could have that kind of a relationship with God. Later I realized that it was the Holy Spirit at work in me, giving me this desire for a close relationship with God. He led me as he leads each of us to offer ourselves entirely to God so that from the depths of our being we can be assured that God accepts us, claiming us as his own.

Make a Decision

If you want to grow closer to God, if you want to be God's man or woman, you must decide to give yourself entirely to him. If you want to participate fully in God's plan, to have the joy of working with him and for him, you must decide to let him occupy the most important place in your life. All that is required for your part is that you desire to let Christ be the Lord of your life. It isn't important to know how this will happen nor how you will be able to overcome the obstacles that will face you in the days and years ahead. Our God is a God of power, and he will show you the way to accomplish his will. For your part, you must honestly yield your own will—submitting your desires to his. Simply make an honest plea, asking God to become the Lord of your life and asking his Spirit to lead you throughout the rest of your life. Growing in a personal relationship with God is not an intellectual matter. If you have not asked God to take charge of your life, then all the information in the world about him will not make you one with God. Your decision and the movement of the Holy Spirit will make it possible for you to grow closer to God. Only after that initial decision will all the discussion, advice, and information that follows be helpful.

If you have never asked the Lord into your life in this way, do it now. And if you have dedicated yourself to the Lord in the past, renew your commitment to him now. Remind yourself how important he is to you. Recommit yourself to serving him no matter what the circumstances. Join together with all those who love God and his Son Jesus Christ and pray with confidence in the power of the Holy Spirit:

> Father in heaven, I acknowledge that you have made me out of nothing. I want to be your servant and to belong to you from now on.
>
> Lord Jesus Christ, I acknowledge that you have redeemed me. I want to belong to you

from now on. I want to be free from darkness and evil, and I want to enter your kingdom and be part of your people. I will turn away from all wrongdoing, and I will avoid anything that leads me to do wrong. I ask you to forgive all the sins I have committed. I offer my life to you, and I promise to obey you as my Lord.

Holy Spirit, I acknowledge that you are the power of the living God. It is you who desires to teach me the truth and to draw me into a deeper relationship with my Lord. Come in power and have your way. Amen.

What Is the Goal?

The goal of our Christian life is to belong entirely to God and to be with him for eternity. There are many ways to describe this goal, each of which can bring out different aspects of it. We can say that we desire to become more like Christ. Each of my children have at one time or other said that they wanted to "grow up to be just like Mom or Dad." Similarly, Christians ought to want to become more like God. This is what Paul was referring to when he said, "I have been crucified with Christ; it is no longer I who live, but Christ who lives in me; and the life I now live in the flesh I live by faith in the Son of God, who loved me and gave himself for me" (Gal 2:20).

Another way to describe our goal is to say that we want to grow into full maturity in Christ. Ephesians 4:13-15 says God's gifts are to equip the saints for building up the body of Christ "until we all attain to the unity of the faith and of the knowledge of the Son of God, to mature manhood, to the measure of the stature of the fulness of Christ; so that we may no longer be children, tossed to and fro and carried about with every wind of doctrine, by the cunning of men, by their craftiness in deceitful wiles. Rather, speaking the truth in love, we are to grow up in every way into him who is the head, into Christ." God does not desire infantile sons and daughters who remain young, immature, and incapable, but, rather, strong and mature men and women, faithful followers who have taken on his mind and who are firmly rooted in Jesus Christ.

A third way to describe the goal of the Christian life is to say that we want to become one with our Christian brothers and sisters. John 17:22-23 quotes Jesus in his final prayer: "The glory which thou hast given me I have given to them, that they may be one even as we are one, I in them and thou in me, that they may become perfectly one, so that the world may know that thou hast sent me and hast loved them even as thou hast loved me." God the Father wants his people to learn to become one, to live out the Christian life in unity with one another.

Other aspects of the goal of the Christian life are pointed out in the Bible—waging spiritual warfare, longing for the kingdom of Christ, and obeying fully the will of God. All these aspects have one thing in common—they focus on something other than ourselves. As we focus our attention on the Lord, on our brothers and sisters, and on people who need the salvation of the Lord, we move toward the goal and are radically changed in the process. We become the kind of persons who can live with and love others. We become more like Christ, bearing his image more clearly. We become useful and consecrated servants of the Master himself.

In Matthew's Gospel, we are told that Jesus was once asked to summarize all of the Old Testament law and prophets. He answered, "You shall love the Lord your God with all your heart, and with all your soul, and with all your mind. This is the great and first commandment. And the second is like it, You shall love your neighbor as yourself. On these two commandments depend all the law and the prophets" (22:35-40). Jesus tells us that the goal of our Christian life can be summed up first by learning to love God entirely and wholeheartedly, and second, by learning to love our neighbor. As we try to grow in our relationship with God and to serve our brothers and sisters in Christian love, we will become different people. We will become more like God, more obviously his sons and daughters.

Is It Possible?

But is it really possible to have this type of relationship with God and with his people? At different times, all of us have probably experienced a lack of desire to pray, difficulty reading the Bible, or the thought that we would much rather be alone than with other Christians. We might be tempted to agree with a young man who once told me that he wasn't sure he wanted to go to heaven because he didn't think he could tolerate having to pray all the time.

It is, in fact, very difficult to love God and your neighbor with all your heart and with all your soul, and to do it consistently. We are not angels but flesh and blood, with bodies that become tired and minds that get distracted. On top of that, we encounter constant opposition from the world, the flesh, and the devil. Even so, we can expect to grow in fulfilling the goals of the Christian life because God understands our limitations and has taken them entirely into account. He does not expect us to be angels, and he has not left us defenseless against his enemies. If we faithfully love and serve him on earth, we will enjoy the great reward of being able to love him without constraint in the hereafter. Until then, we are to resist discouragement and to strive for this goal with the help of the Lord.

Of course we can gain practical wisdom that can help us deal with specific difficulties as we grow in our relationship with the Lord, but for now it is enough to ask the Lord himself to help us experience his presence more consistently. On our part we must promise to faithfully seek him. Scripture tells us repeatedly that if we seek the Lord he will be found. We are told that we will recognize his voice like sheep who know the shepherd's voice. We are told that Jesus will help us to draw close to God. Jesus himself said, "And I will pray the Father, and he will give you another Counselor, to be with you for ever, even the Spirit of truth, whom the world cannot receive, because it neither sees him nor knows him; you know him, for he dwells with you, and will be in you. I will not leave you desolate; I will come to you" (Jn 14:16-18).

But wouldn't it be easier to love and follow God if Jesus himself were still with us to talk to us, to encourage and lead us. Apparently not. Jesus knew that it would be more profitable if God were to dwell within each one of us, so he said, "It is to your advantage that I go away, for if I do not go away, the Counselor will not come to you; but if I go, I will send him to you. . . . When the Spirit of truth comes, he will guide you into all the truth" (Jn 16:7, 13). In fact, Jesus promises that both he and the Father will themselves live in our hearts if we desire them to and if we keep his commands. "If a man loves me, he will keep my word, and my Father will love him, and we will come to him and make our home with him" (Jn 14:23). Through the action of the Holy Spirit, the Father and the Son will live with us, helping us to be one with them.

Is it really possible to achieve the goal of becoming one with God, serving him and his people with our whole heart and soul and mind? Not if we attempt to do it relying on our own strength and determination, for man cannot save himself. But as Jesus said, when the disciples once asked him who could be saved, "With men it is impossible, but not with God; for all things are possible with God" (Mk 10:27). We must hear God's call to us to live a life of daily dedication, and we must respond by saying, "Yes, Lord. I'm available. Let it be so." We must learn what our part involves so that God can produce in us thirty, sixty, and a hundredfold fruitfulness. We must believe that God's goal for us is indeed possible, even when we don't seem to possess all the resources we need. God is a God who takes what we offer and multiplies it until it far exceeds our expectation. "Give, and it will be given to you; good measure, pressed down, shaken together, running over, will be put into your lap. For the measure you give will be the measure you get back" (Lk 6:38).

TWO

Building a Relationship with God

I ONCE GAVE a talk on the topic of caring for wives to a group which included both single and married men. During the talk I mentioned some of the ways in which a husband should care for his wife. I spoke about how important it is to encourage, appreciate, and honor her, overseeing the host of planning and problem-solving efforts she makes on behalf of the whole family.

Afterwards, one of the single men told me that he agreed with the theory of my talk. But it seemed to him like a lot of hard work to put the theory into practice. What he hadn't realized was that in a good Christian marriage, the practice is easier than the theory because the husband loves the wife. I told him that during the early years of my marriage to Ellen, I had naturally looked for ways to show her my love. I found it easy to spend time with her, to talk with her, and to serve her. Over the ensuing years, this initial spontaneous care had developed into a pattern of relating that included all of these important aspects of our relationship.

The same holds true for our relationship with

God. When we first come to the Lord, we often experience a deep inner desire to show him our love. We express this by praying to him, thinking about him, and talking about him to others. The Holy Spirit seems able to use our first love, whether natural or spiritual, to inflame in us a desire to do what is right. Even after we have known and served the Lord faithfully for many years, the Holy Spirit will still be able to keep our first love alive if we have incorporated these right ways of relating into our regular pattern of life. In Revelation 2:4 the Spirit says, "But I have this against you, that you have abandoned the love you had at first." Clearly, God wants us to maintain our first love for him, even as it matures, becoming deeper and more solid.

Listen, then, to what the Spirit of God says to you. You have already decided to allow Christ to direct your life. Now open your heart, yield to the Lord, and decide to make the Lord God your first and deepest love. Decide to live your life for him and to work for love of him. Decide that you want a deeper relationship with the Lord. Commit yourself to him and let the Holy Spirit lead you in your relationship with God.

Learning How

One summer I was working in the garage with my two-year-old son, Daniel, changing the tire on one of our bicycles. Danny watched me as I took tools from my toolbox and began to repair the bike. After a while Danny picked up a wrench and started banging on one of the pedals in an attempt to imitate me. He has always had a desire to work alongside me, and I was glad we were together as father and son. His enthusiasm for the job was impressive, but his random banging didn't help much. In a similar way, our heavenly Father is delighted that we desire to improve our relationship with him, but he expects us to learn how to use the various tools that will help us to do that.

We need to learn some practical ways of growing in our relationship with the Lord. In order to successfully incorporate something new into your life, three elements are necessary. First, you need to become acquainted with the area you are trying to change. Second, you must consciously accept the need for the change and the methods required to bring about the change. Third, you must apply what you have learned until the change comes about. Most of us have failed in one or more of these areas as we have tried to grow in our spiritual life.

Four basic tools form an essential part of God's plan for his people—prayer, study, service, and fellowship. The Christian life could be pictured as a wheel, the rim of which represents daily Christian living, and the hub of which is the Lord Jesus Christ himself, the source of power for every aspect of our lives. A wheel is constructed in such as way that power is transmitted from the hub to the rim through the spokes. If the wheel is the Christian life and Christ is the hub, then the spokes that transmit the power of Jesus to us are prayer, study, service, and fellowship. All of these are critical means by which our whole life is put into contact with Jesus, allowing him to empower and transform it according to his plan. The remainder of this book will discuss each of these elements in order for us to understand how to incorporate them into our daily Christian life.

THREE

Learning to Pray

DAILY PRAYER is the single, most fundamental means of growth available to us. This isn't too surprising if you think about it. We are trying to develop a personal relationship with God. Like any other personal relationship, it will grow in proportion to the time we invest in it.

I was reminded of this lesson when my oldest child, Debbie, started attending school. At first I made no special effort to talk with her to find out what was happening at school. I didn't pay any particular attention until I began to notice her saying and doing things that made me ask myself, "Where did she pick that up?" I began to realize that it was important for her to talk to me daily about her school experiences so that I could help her to understand them and successfully pass on to her a Christian perspective about the knowledge she was gaining. Since our goal is to become like God in our character, we, too, must spend time with him daily, telling him our thoughts and learning from him the truths of his kingdom.

One of the great revelations of Christianity is that God himself wants to have a personal relationship with each of us. We certainly could never have expected that God, in his immensity, would want to listen to our every prayer, even the small ones. And yet Jesus has told us that we are to call God "Father." I remember attending a business meeting that was interrupted by a phone call from one man's five-year-old son. The little boy was distraught because his bicycle had just been crushed in the driveway by the family car. The father took time to advise and comfort the son, and none of us begrudged him the time. Clearly, the boy needed his father and his need took precedence. That's how it often is with us.

We need to spend time daily with God in prayer in order to give our relationship with him a chance to grow. Prayer is the special means of interaction that is reserved for those who love God, and it gives great delight to God when we come to him in this way.

Setting Priorities

Even though we may want to pray regularly, we can experience difficulty settling down and actually praying. I remember the first time I learned the difference between wanting to do something and actually doing it. As a young boy I wanted to buy a basket for my bike, so I decided I had to find a way to earn some money. I convinced our next-door neighbor to hire me to mow his lawn once a week during the summer. I cut his lawn that same day, still enthused about having my first paying job. But the next week I procrastinated several times, and my neighbor had to have a talk with me to get me to commit myself to a time and day on which I would cut the lawn. In the same way it doesn't work for us to say to the Lord, "I really want to pray but I don't have time right now. But later I'll pray for sure." God could respond by saying, "You have been first in all my thoughts; have I been first in all your thoughts? I have in every way come to you; have you in every way come to me? I have poured myself out to you, and given myself to you without reserve; have you given yourself entirely to me? Seek me. I have already sought you. Look to me. Make me first in your lives."

We need to make a practical decision to pray at a specific time each day. For some people the best time will be in the morning, before they become deeply involved in the day's activities. Others will prefer to pray at lunchtime or in the evening. Mothers of young children might need to pray before the children rise, while they are taking naps, or after they go to sleep in the evening. Whatever time you decide is best, decide to stick to it by making it part of your daily schedule. But, you might ask, won't scheduled prayer be too structured an approach? Won't it dampen the spontaneity I need for prayer? On the contrary. By making your prayer time a priority and making sure that it fits in your schedule, you will be in a better position to develop a warm, strong relationship with God. Consider, for instance, the bone structure of your body—rigid and clearly defined, and yet the very thing that allows you great freedom of movement. So it is with a scheduled time for prayer.

Since so much of our daily activity is run according to a schedule (work hours, store hours, television programs, and so on) and since so many pressures are on us to produce and meet deadlines, any unscheduled activity will soon be crowded out and replaced by other activities, no matter how strong your initial commitment may be.

Once you decide on a time of day that works best in your list of daily activities, don't be disturbed if it is sometimes impossible to pray at that time. Some conflicts are inevitable. However, such days will be fewer than you think if you decide to build your day's activities upon prayer, to schedule it into your work, and to make the effort to persist in it.

Practical Steps

After I decided to make prayer a priority in life and began to pray daily, many practical questions arose. Just how should I pray? How long should I pray? Am I being legalistic? Am I being sincere if I pray when I don't feel like it? How should I use scripture in my prayer time? Should I have a prayer list? Should I pray out loud? Should I stand or kneel? Should I dance with joy?

Books on prayer usually do not answer practical questions like these because an approach that works well for one person may be a big distraction for someone else. Therefore, many authors try to limit themselves to general rules which will prove helpful to everyone.

However, I think it is worth discussing these practical details because it is so helpful to know how someone else has answered the questions we face in our own efforts to pray. I intend to describe several methods of prayer that have proved helpful either to me or to other people I know. I offer these as a fund of examples and information rather than as a specific plan of action. Certainly no one should consider implementing all or even most of these ideas at once in their prayer life. Nor will every one of the items discussed prove helpful to you right now. But it can help to have some practical models in mind as you let God's Holy Spirit form your own approach to prayer.

The traditional way to learn prayer is to learn it from a man of prayer whom you trust. In the time of Jesus, people became disciples of holy men who could teach them the truths about God and the ways to God. We see this in Luke's Gospel. One of Jesus' disciples came to him and said, "Lord, teach us to pray, as John taught his disciples." Likewise, the best way for you to learn to pray is to talk about prayer with someone you respect, someone who has a strong and vital prayer life. I encourage you to discuss the information in this section with someone you can trust to help you apply it properly.

A strong Christian tradition exists in which

each day is begun in prayer as a way of dedicating the whole day to God. In Psalm 5 King David says, "O LORD, in the morning thou dost hear my voice; in the morning I prepare a sacrifice for thee, and watch" (Ps 5:3). Two thousand years later, Jesus kept the same early morning watch: "And in the morning, a great while before day, he rose and went out to a lonely place, and there he prayed" (Mk 1:35). Throughout Christian history, from the apostles to Mother Teresa of Calcutta, strong men and women have been known for their dedication to daily prayer and their habit of rising early to pray. A dedication to prayer characterized the lives of the Christians of early centuries, the great leaders of both Eastern and Western Christianity, and the lives of the Reformers. Even in our day the people who inspire us most are often people of prayer.

Matthew Henry is quoted as saying, "Let prayer be the key of the morning and the bolt of the evening." I myself have experienced the wisdom of this approach. Whenever I have plunged directly into the day's activities without first spending time in prayer, I have quickly forgotten about God as I work and become more independent in my efforts. My wife, too, has noticed a direct connection between beginning her day in prayer and the ability to peacefully carry out her responsibilities throughout the rest of the day. She has been particularly inspired by the story of John Wesley's mother, Susanna, who was known as a woman of prayer, all the more impressive when you realize that she raised nineteen children to know and serve God.

My morning prayer time has become an essential element of my daily schedule. In order to build morning prayer into my schedule, I have taken a two-fold approach. First, I have made a habit of praying as I awake and prepare for work in the morning. Immediately upon rising I thank the Lord for giving me another day in which to serve him. I simply say, "Thank you, Lord. Help me to serve you well another day." While washing and shaving I may sing a short Christian song, pray some traditional prayers, or recall some scripture verses that I have memorized. One passage that has served well for this purpose is Colossians 3:23, "Whatever your task, work heartily, as serving the Lord and not men, knowing that from the Lord you will receive the inheritance as your reward; you are serving the Lord Christ." Another is from Psalm 100: "Make a joyful noise to the Lord, all the lands! Serve the Lord with gladness! Come into his presence with singing! Know that the Lord is God! It is he that made us, and we are his; we are his people, and the sheep of his pasture. Enter his gates with thanksgiving, and his courts with praise! Give thanks to him, bless his name! For the Lord is good; his steadfast love endures forever, and his faithfulness to all generations."

During the first five or ten minutes after waking, my mind tends to run along whatever path it is started upon. I used to find myself repeating advertising jingles in my mind or getting bogged down thinking about the problems I would have to face later in the day. But now I find that singing, or reciting scripture, or praying simple prayers are much more rewarding and better ways to establish my mind on the Lord.

After dressing and eating, I take a longer period of time to pray and read scripture. It helps to pray in an isolated room far away from sleeping children or other people in the house. This allows me to sing a song, perhaps accompanied by a guitar (though not everyone appreciates guitars), and to take an initial ten-minute period of time to praise God out loud. Often during this time I will pray one of the psalms aloud, and if I come across some verses of praise I will repeat them or chant them, allowing them to inspire me in personal praise of God. After that initial period of praise, I take five or ten minutes to talk to God about the particular needs of the day and about the ongoing concerns on my prayer list. This list contains both serious needs, like prayers for some friends whose marriage is dissolving, and smaller needs, like help to complete a work project on time.

While praying like this I try to avoid having a one-sided conversation with the Lord. I once heard a friend say that he was taught from an early age how to talk to God but didn't learn that he could listen to God until he was forty! So I try to remain sensitive to the Holy Spirit so that God has a chance to direct me by inspiration, spiritual senses, or specific scripture passages.

It is not always possible to be perfectly alert

during prayer. Whenever I realize that my mind has wandered, I simply return it to prayer. God knows what it is to be human, and I am convinced that he allows for such natural things. Of course, it is wise to avoid praying in a place filled with objects that can easily distract you and to avoid praying at a time when you are likely to be interrupted. If you find that some particular concern is returning to your mind repeatedly, it may be best to pray about that concern rather than treat it as a distraction to be avoided. On certain days, when I am very busy or when many questions or ideas come to mind during my time of prayer, I have kept a pencil and paper at hand to write down items that occur to me. Having written them down, I can forget them until later.

I remember the story of how God called David Wilkerson to leave the pastoral work he was doing in a small country church and enter a whole new type of inner-city work in New York City. God spoke to him in simple steps. First God impressed him with the conviction that he needed to spend more time in prayer. He tried to dismiss the idea because he thought it was impossible in light of his busy schedule. But finally he decided to stop watching late-night television so that he could rise early to pray. When he began to do this faithfully, God then led him, a step at a time, into a new and completely unexpected ministry. If we give God a little room to deal with us, he will take full advantage of it to direct our lives according to his plan.

Most often I take the final ten minutes of my morning prayer time to read scripture, again being alert to anything that might stand out to me from the reading. Sometimes I stop at a verse that strikes me and praise God as I repeat the verse or take time to meditate on its meaning for me. After getting the most out of that particular verse I continue reading scripture, allowing a minute or so at the end to evaluate what I have learned in the course of the reading. Then I try to think of one practical way to implement that lesson during the course of the upcoming day.

In short, many people have found it valuable to make God the first thought on their mind each morning in order to dedicate the day to his service. After turning their thoughts to God at the outset of the day, they then take a little longer prayer time. Even if this requires rising earlier, it may well prove to be a worthwhile way to help you incorporate fruitful daily prayer into your schedule.

FOUR

Ways of Praying

QUESTIONS ARISE about how to go about spending time with the Lord each day in prayer. It can help to think of our prayer time as composed of three different categories of prayer: giving, asking, and receiving. *Giving* to God includes prayers of praise, adoration, and thanksgiving, and the singing of spiritual songs. These are all ways of acknowledging God as our Creator, deserving of praise from his people. The prayers of scripture are full of examples of praise, thanksgiving, and adoration. The psalms contain examples of all the basic types of prayer and are filled throughout with statements like "Praise the Lord; Not to us, O Lord, not to us, but to thy name give glory; Great are the works of the Lord; O give thanks to the Lord for he is good; Bless the Lord, O my soul, and all that is within me bless his holy name; Sing to the Lord, bless his name, tell of his salvation from day to day." This is the sacrifice of praise that we are commanded to give to the Lord. One of the main reasons we pray is to give God the praise and glory he deserves.

Scripture also tells us to *ask* God to take care of the needs of others. In fact, we are commanded and encouraged to ask and we are reprimanded for not asking. In many of his epistles, the apostle Paul asks that his fellow Christians pray that he might be able to successfully preach the gospel in the places where God sends him. In Ephesians 6:19, he instructs the Christians at Ephesus to "pray at all times in the Spirit, with all prayer and supplication. To that end keep alert with all perseverance, while making supplication for all the saints, and also for me." In 1 Timothy 2:1 Paul again urges that supplications, prayers, intercessions, and thanksgivings be made for all men and also for kings and others in high positions so that Christians might be allowed to live a quiet, peaceable life, godly and respectful in every way. And of course scripture abounds with examples of prayers for people who are sick, for people to come to believe the gospel of Jesus, and for fellow believers who are sinning. This type of asking, interceding for the needs of others, should form an important part of our prayer.

Scripture also encourages us to bring our personal petitions before the Lord. The Bible speaks of God as one who knows our needs and who will supply them when we ask. Jesus tells us that if we ask it will be given to us and if we seek we will find the answers to our prayers. He says, "For everyone who asks receives, and he who seeks finds, and to him who knocks it will be opened to him" (Lk 11:10). Furthermore, it appears that Jesus wants us to be bold and confident, to persevere in asking for God's will to be accomplished. He prefaces his promise with the story of a man who went to a friend at midnight, asking for three loaves of bread in order to feed an unexpected visitor. Jesus says, "I tell you, though he will not get up and give him anything because he is his friend, yet because of his importunity he will rise and give him whatever he needs. And I tell you, Ask and it will be given you" (Lk 11:8-9). Jesus' last words to his disciples, reported in John 14-16, were that they should ask the Father and ask in the name of the Son. Jesus' words are repeated seven times in these three chapters. James says it plainly: "You do not have, because you do not ask. You ask and do not receive, because you ask wrongly, to spend it on your passions" (Jas 4:2-4). Clearly, asking for legitimate needs—to live peaceably, to meet our responsibilities, and to spread the gospel—should constitute a normal element of our prayer life.

You can make these kinds of petitions regularly by taking a bit of time to pray each day for your personal needs and for the needs of others, especially those for whom you have some responsibility. Try keeping a list of major needs for which you pray. This will help you remember items to pray for, and it will help you notice when specific prayers have been answered. Jesus once healed ten lepers, but only one returned to thank him. It is our responsibility to notice and give thanks for answered prayers.

The summer we built our house, I realized how easy it is to forget to be thankful. The list of needs grew daily—first buy the land, then survey it, then get it annexed, then hope for dry weather during rough-in, then pass the inspection, and on and on. Whenever one goal was achieved, two more crowded in to replace it. It seemed to me that we were engaged in an uphill battle, and I could see no end to it. But then I realized that I was losing perspective. As soon as I began to thank God after each prayer was answered, my whole outlook changed. I began to appreciate the progress that had been made and to realize that I was part of a team with God, meeting the challenges one at a time with his help. Being thankful builds our faith, making it easier for us to believe that God will answer other prayer requests.

However, we should never approach praying for our needs in a legalistic fashion. We should not feel obligated to pray for every possible need but only for those things for which God has made us responsible, or those things that he has drawn our attention to pray for. I sometimes imagine the Holy Spirit telling different people to pray for different aspects of God's plan so that a broad spectrum of people can join with God in the joy of seeing his will fulfilled. It is important to resist the tendency to spend all of your prayer time interceding. Instead, you should intercede faithfully, a little every day. It's also important to be specific in your prayers whenever possible. That way you will have a better idea of when and how God is answering your prayers.

One final principle involves responding to specific prayer requests. Whenever anyone used to ask me to pray for some particular need of theirs, I would always say yes. When I did this, one of two things usually happened. I would either forget to pray and then feel guilty, or else I would remember to add their name to my prayer list but then wonder how much to pray for them or how long to continue. I began to understand that I was to pray regularly and diligently only for those things which God assigned to me, and to say a simpler prayer for other concerns. After that, whenever anyone would ask me to pray for something, I would stop right there in the conversation and say, "Yes, that's a good idea. Let's pray now." If possible I would take a moment to pray with them then and there. After that, I would only pray for that particular need if it was brought to my attention again or if I sensed the Lord giving it to me as an ongoing responsibility. This approach has proved a great protection, and it has allowed me to pray for many more people than I was ever able to before.

The third element of prayer involves *receiving from God,* both spiritually and materially. Spiritually, we need to expect that the Holy Spirit will lead us, guide us, direct us, encourage us, and teach us during the time that we set aside to pray. We should expect the Holy Spirit to teach us about God, what he's like, what he desires, what pleases him and what displeases him, what he expects of us, and how he reacts in different situations. Of course, much of our knowledge of God comes to us through other Christians. But God also speaks directly, providing for our needs. As we grow in our relationship with God, we should grow in our ability to hear his still, small voice in our hearts.

One practical way to listen to God is to wait silently in his presence. Certainly our prayer times should not always be entirely silent or meditative. Yet we should learn a kind of fruitful and productive way to rest in the presence of God. The psalmist says, "I will wait on thy name. . . . My soul waiteth upon God" (Ps 52:9 and 62:11, KJV) and "My soul waits for the LORD more than watchmen for the morning" (Ps 130:6). We are told that they that wait upon the Lord shall renew their strength (Is 40:31). And so we should allow ourselves to remain silent in the presence of the Lord, not daydreaming, or making lists in our mind, or carrying on a monologue with God, but recognizing God's presence and surrendering ourselves to him. We wait before God as his creatures, who love him and are at his disposal. Such waiting may well lead to other forms of prayer, including strong outward praise. But we wait because it expresses a genuine part of our relationship with God. Most of us should not expect to strive for long periods of meditative silence before the Lord. For most people this is not an easy form of prayer. But we should expect to grow in our ability to hear God.

A second way to help us listen to the Lord during our prayer time is to meditate on scripture. In Psalm 19:14, David prays that the words of his mouth and the meditation of his heart would be acceptable in the sight of God, his redeemer. And Psalm 119 speaks of meditating on God's law, on his precepts, on his ways. Meditation is simply taking one specific aspect of our Christian life and thinking about it prayerfully, allowing the Holy Spirit to teach or inspire us about the topic. Paul encourages us in Philippians 4:8 to do this: "Finally, brethren, whatever is true, whatever is honorable, whatever is just, whatever is pure, whatever is lovely, whatever is gracious, if there is any excellence, if there is anything worthy of praise, think about these things."

Sometimes I meditate on an event from the gospels, like the healing of the withered man's hand on the Sabbath, as described in the third chapter of Mark. I picture the people and the events, asking myself what happened in this situation. Why did people address each other the way they did? What do their answers to Jesus show about their spiritual understanding of who he was? What would I have done in a similar situation? How could I apply this passage to my own life?

Or I might meditate on one of the instructions from the epistles, such as Philippians 4:11-12, which says, "Not that I complain of want; for I have learned, in whatever state I am, to be content. I know how to be abased, and I know how to abound; in any and all circumstances I have learned the secret of facing plenty and hunger, abundance and want." I try to understand the passage as well as I can, reading it as many as four or five times, in more than one translation. I write down any questions that occur to me about the passage, especially things that I do not understand or that I find difficult to accept. I tell the Lord in prayer that I desire to both understand and accept his word in my life and pray that he will help me to do that. My goal here is not intellectual knowledge but spiritual understanding. Many times I will gain one or two insights simply as a result of letting the Holy Spirit work with me during the meditation. I always try to remember to thank the Lord for what he has shown me and to think of some simple, practical way to apply what I've just learned to my activities in the coming day.

A third practical way of listening to the Lord is to remain alert to the spiritual realities that are going on in the circumstances of our life. Jesus in the garden of Gethsemane invited his disciples to come and watch with him for an hour. The word watch means to be awake or vigilant or on guard. We need to keep a clear vision of the spiritual realities amidst which we live. Paul says we are not fighting flesh and blood but principalities and spiritual powers. Sometimes, as you pray about various things in your life, God will give you an insight or a spiritual sense that will help you see the situation from his perspective.

Very often, we make the mistake of praying with the mindset that communication is one way only—us speaking to God. In this case God is not able to give us these kinds of insights. But if, instead, we stay alert, expecting God to communicate with us during our prayer time, we will be able to receive direction from him as well as to give him the praise he deserves. This happened in a striking way a year ago when my wife and I purchased land with three other families, intending to build houses near one another. We had sold one of our houses already and hired a friend named Dave as the builder. As we went through the formalities of trying to annex the land into the city so that we could get permits to build on it some serious obstacles arose, and it began to look like we could lose the mortgage promised to us. It an anxious time and I remember praying that God would spare us from financial and legal troubles.

I very distinctly felt the urge to open the Bible that was on the table before me, and as I did my eyes fell upon 1 Chronicles 15:1, "David built houses for himself in the city." It was a startling and joyful passage that encouraged all of us at that tense moment. And today when I look out my front door and see all the houses completed, I still thank God for speaking so clearly when we needed it. Of course this wasn't the original meaning of the passage, but God sometimes uses scripture to speak a personal word to people.

If you think that God is giving you significant

direction in your prayer time, you should test it against scripture, relying on wisdom and the input of other Christians whom you can trust. But by all means expect the Holy Spirit to lead, guide, and anoint you in your prayer time.

A few words about various methods of prayer will help at this point. I have found that no one approach to prayer works all of the time. Variety and flexibility are essential principles for someone who has decided to pray every day regardless of how they feel. My approach normally balances silent and vocal prayer, spontaneous and traditional prayer, and giving and receiving from the Lord. But if on a particular day it seems right to engage in more loud praise and singing than usual, I feel free to do so. I may even continue that way throughout the week, or for as long as it seems helpful. Throughout my prayer time I am always open to doing something a little differently if it will help. And so I am free to stand and walk around, to kneel, or even at times to lay prostrate during prayer. At times I pray and read scripture out loud, while at other times I meditate quietly. Some days I read large chunks of scripture or do other spiritual reading. On other days, I repeat one verse over and over. I don't try to change my style of prayer each day, but I am open to modifying it if necessary and to continue with the new approach as long as seems helpful.

To maintain this kind of flexibility, you will need to find a time and place in which you are free to pray in the various ways mentioned. If there are days when nothing seems appealing and no method seems to work well, then simply follow the principle of faithfulness—pray anyway, but pray!

Remember, we do not pray to please ourselves but to please God. We do it because he wants us to, because it is our duty. Many times our daily prayer time will seem like a great benefit to us, but even when it doesn't, we should worship the Lord faithfully.

Effective Intercession

For the last three years I have led a group of people committed to daily intercessory prayer. One thing we have all learned is that it can be difficult to intercede properly. Sometimes our petitions tend to take over our regular prayer time, particularly when many pressing needs come to our attention at once. At other times, we find ourselves avoiding intercession because we have not seen answers to our prayers. But we do our best to steer clear of such extremes and to keep intercession in the proper perspective. Intercession is something God wants us to do; in fact, it is a privilege. Intercession is not so much a way of getting answers as it is an opportunity to cooperate intimately in fulfilling God's plan. Of course, God does want to answer our prayers, and we should make specific personal requests as well as intercede for larger, more universal needs (like peace, Christian unity, and so on). But we should not forget that the privilege of bringing our needs freely to God is as important as the answered prayers. And while it may be simple enough to ask for something once, it is much more challenging to make intercession a regular part of our life. I received a note from one of the members of the intercessors' group that illustrates this point well. She was writing about some of the things God was doing in her life.

> During the past six weeks, I've experienced an increased urgency about the necessity of intercession. Very frequently I've experienced promptings to intercede at different times during the day, but in the different situations I had some difficulty knowing how to intercede while still continuing with the task at hand. And at the same time that I have experienced the increased urgency and desire to intercede, I have also experienced increasing distractions in prayer and a practical difficulty in finding the time to pray. It has been a struggle.

Such struggles are common when you are learning how to intercede effectively, but don't become discouraged. Jesus has invited and commanded his followers to intercede, and he himself carries our petitions to the throne of God where "he always lives to make intercession" (Heb 7:25).

It can be difficult to know how to pray in any given situation. Our lack of understanding can prevent us from making clear, bold prayers of intercession. I experienced this very clearly in a hospital room in Washington, D.C. It was just after Christmas, and I was praying for a friend of mine named Rosemary. She had been hospitalized for cancer and at that moment was in a coma. The doctor told me he didn't think she would live through the night. Rosemary had lived her forty-eight years firmly and fully depending on Jesus and witnessing the truth of the gospel to many people. Even throughout her hospitalization, she knew that the Lord could heal her instantly, and she communicated her trust to the patients and staff around her. Now she lay in a coma, breathing with great difficulty. And I really did not know how to pray for her. If she were healed, it would be a marvel to the doctors. No doubt she could draw many people to God through her story. But if she were to die, she would be with Jesus and would therefore have the better part. I asked God to give me specific guidance as I held her hand and prayed, but I had no clear sense of how he wanted me to pray at that moment. So I stopped trying to formulate a specific petition and simply stood there in God's presence, praying that his will be done. There was a certain peace that was present for about fifteen or twenty minutes. Then Rosemary gave a small gasp and stopped breathing. And suddenly, almost as if God were showing me what was happening in the heavenly places, I sensed her spirit passing from my hands into heaven. I knew at that moment what God's plan was for Rosemary.

After Rosemary's death, I recalled Paul's words

in Romans: "Likewise the Spirit helps us in our weakness; for we do not know how to pray as we ought, but the Spirit himself intercedes for us with sighs too deep for words" (Rom 8:26). The passage goes on to say that the Spirit intercedes for the saints according to the will of God. God knows that there will be many times when we do not know how to pray as we ought. And yet we will want to join with God and make our prayer available for his use. We should be able to intercede regularly for all our needs, big and small, asking the Holy Spirit to help us intercede according to the perfect will of God.

Keeping a Prayer Notebook

Many books on prayer recommend keeping a prayer notebook. This is not something that works well for everyone, but for some people it can be very helpful if done in the right way. A fruitful prayer time will often produce questions or ideas for future meditation, inspirational passages worth remembering, and sometimes even correction or exhortation from the Lord. God may sometimes deal with you for several days, or even weeks, about the same subject, and it is only the sum of all his dealings that reveal the whole picture. It can help to write down some of these things. But don't just grab a scrap of paper, make a note on it, and tuck it away with other notes in the pages of your Bible. Chances are that you will never use these loose notes again because they are not ordered in any way. All that this kind of note-taking results in is an overstuffed Bible. It works better to have a special notebook in which to write down these thoughts.

In the pamphlet entitled, "How to Have a Daily Quiet Time," Larry Christenson offers his suggestions for how to use a prayer notebook. He says, "Write down what comes to you during this reading-meditation-praying time. This is the key to your whole quiet time. When you write it down, you begin to crystalize and capture the actual workings of the Holy Spirit in your heart, mind, and soul. Make it quite personal and direct. Not simply what the passage 'means,' but what it means to you and for you. Perhaps it will trigger some thought not directly related to the passage you are reading. That's alright. Write it down. This is the Holy Spirit's personal message to you."

I have kept such a prayer notebook off and on during the last fourteen years, and in the process have discovered some advantages and some drawbacks. One unexpected advantage is that my notebook has helped me to realize whether I have been faithful to my daily prayer time. More than once, as I have reviewed my notebook, I've been surprised to discover that during busy times I have sometimes neglected to pray for two, three, and even four days in a row. During busy and stressful periods of life, we need to draw closer to God, and yet it is precisely at those times that we find it hardest to pray faithfully. A friend of mine recently met some women who work directly with

Mother Teresa of Calcutta. They told him that Mother Teresa has always been very faithful about praying daily, but that after she received the Nobel Peace Prize, she decided to double the amount of time she spent in daily prayer. Likewise, when our responsibilities increase, our prayer time should increase, and when we get busy, we should be even more diligent in giving time to the Lord. Keeping a notebook can indicate just how faithful we are at daily prayer.

There are certain pitfalls to avoid when keeping a prayer notebook. Remember that your notebook is supposed to be an asset to your prayer time, not a distraction. It is easy to pay too much attention to the grammar, neatness, or completeness of your notebook, almost as though you were writing a book for future generations. To counteract this tendency, I have at times decided to make my notes short and cryptic, so that only I can understand them. At other times I have stopped keeping notes during my prayer time. You may need to take similar steps to be sure that you are spending your prayer time praying instead of writing a book. Your goal should be to use your notebook to record major ideas or passages that you think will be helpful to review or study later.

How much time should you spend reviewing what God has spoken to you in previous prayer times? I have known people who spend part of their prayer time each week reviewing what they have written in their prayer notebook. At first this sounded like a virtuous, studious thing to do. But I never seemed to have the time or discipline to do it and found myself making good resolutions to begin a weekly review "someday" in the future. But when I mentioned it to a friend, he made an interesting comment. "I think you need to realize, Tom," he said, that prayer is not primarily for your sake, but is primarily a service to God. You shouldn't be spending a large part of your prayer time in self-examination." As I thought about this principle afterwards, I began to realize how valuable it was. Worship in both Old and New Testaments was based on God's worth. Sacrifice was offered to him because he was worthy of it. Certainly we benefit from our prayer and so do others. But our primary goal is to worship God, not to work out all our problems.

Therefore, resist the temptation to use your notebook as a tool for self-analysis. If you want to use your prayer notebook as a means of reviewing what God has been doing and saying to you, do it only once or twice a year, possibly around your birthday or at the start of a new year. These are natural times for reflecting about the past and the future. Doing a review then can remind you of unfinished business that you should focus on in the upcoming year. Used in this way, the orderly notes you make in your prayer time can be a helpful tool without becoming the main focus of your efforts.

Pray Constantly

The question I am asked most frequently is "How much time should I spend in prayer each day?" A simple rule of thumb is to pray the length of time that works in your daily schedule. Your prayer time should be longer than ten minutes because it probably takes you that long to wake up in the morning or to settle your mind in the evening. A half hour is a good goal to aim for. Many people who have been taking a daily prayer time for years find it works very well for them to pray from thirty minutes to an hour each day. But the real answer to the question doesn't consist of the precise number of minutes to be spent in prayer each day. In fact, the New Testament issues certain mysterious commands to pray constantly and unceasingly. In Ephesians 6:18, St. Paul says, "Pray at all times in the Spirit, with all prayer and supplication." Again in 1 Thessalonians 5:16 he says, "Rejoice always, pray constantly, give thanks in all circumstances; for this is will of God in Christ Jesus for you."

Verses like these seem impossible to understand fully. Indeed, they are part of the Christian mystery, which our intellects cannot fully grasp and of which there can be no one, simple explanation. These verses might represent an invitation to begin to enter here on earth into the activity that will come so naturally to us in heaven! If you have ever set aside a day to pray and draw closer to God, you know how refreshing it can be. It may be that scripture includes commands like these because the Lord wants us to strive to make constant prayer part of our daily Christian lives.

Of course, the principles we have already discussed can help us fulfill this command in part by integrating the ongoing elements of prayer into our day: dedicating the day upon rising; taking time in the morning or evening for extended prayer and devotional scripture reading; studying scripture; interceding alone and with others; and joining with other Christians for group prayer and worship. As all of these elements begin to work together in our daily life, they will help us to put the Lord at the forefront of our minds. Yet we should not stop here. All this adds up to only forty-five minutes or an hour spread throughout each day. As such, it represents an incomplete response to the command to pray constantly.

I would like to suggest two additional ways of trying to implement this concept of constant prayer into your prayer life. The first involves increasing your awareness of the presence of God in your life, and the second involves taking short times at various hours of the day to pray.

The first way to make constant prayer a reality in our lives involves raising our awareness of the Holy Spirit's presence within us. If we truly understand that we are temples of the Holy Spirit, we will realize that God is with us wherever we are. Even if we sometimes do not experience him during the course of our day, he has not forgotten or abandoned us. If our clear aim is to love and serve God in all of our daily pursuits, we can be in a sense "praying constantly" as we go about our work. This approach does not separate prayer from the other activities we do, but rather places our whole life within the framework of prayer. Such prayer is sometimes expressed verbally and sometimes through work and service. This concept is expressed in the literature and proverbs of many cultures. John Whittier talked about making life a prayer. An old Latin proverb, *ora et labora,* is translated "pray and work." Augustine said, "He who labors, prays." Bernard said, "He who prays and labors lifts his heart to God with his hands." And an old Russian proverb also linked prayer and work: "Pray to God, but keep the hammer going."

A story is told about an early Christian, Lucius of Enna, one of the men who lived a life of prayer and meditation in the deserts of Egypt in the second century A.D. Younger men, called "men of prayer," came to the old man once to question him about prayer. Lucius asked them what kind of labor they did, and they proudly answered that they did not work, but as the apostles commanded they prayed without ceasing. The old man decided to teach them a lesson about what it means to pray without ceasing. He questioned them with mock surprise, asking how they could live without eating or sleeping, to which they replied that they did both. Who, he asked them, prayed for them while they ate and while they slept? They could find no answer. Then he went on to explain to them how he fulfilled the command to pray constantly. He said that during the day he worked with his hands, weaving a few palm leaves into mats and all the while praying the scripture verse from Psalm 51, "Have mercy on me, O God, according to thy steadfast love; according to thy abundant mercy block out my transgressions." Then he sold the mats for about sixteen denarii, out of which he spent fourteen for the day's food and placed two at the entrance of his hut. He went on, "Whoever finds the two denarii prays for me while I sleep and eat; and so by God's grace there is fulfilled in me the scripture which says, 'Pray without ceasing' " (*The Desert Fathers* by Helen Waddell, 1971, Ann Arbor Paperbacks, The University of Michigan Press, p. 112). The old man's story teaches us that human beings are not made to be able to focus constantly on prayer throughout the day. But if we make it our intention to serve God and not man (Eph 6:7), we can know that our labor pleases the Lord and that it can be offered to him as acceptable worship.

The Old Testament instructs God's people to worship him by sacrificing a portion of the fruit of their labors—animals from their flocks, cereals from their grains, and oil and wine from their presses. In the New Testament, this offering is expanded to include not just part of our produce, but all that we are and everything we do. We actually can offer ourself as a "living sacrifice, holy and acceptable to God, which is your spiritual worship" (Rom 12:1). In *Essays on Prayer,* A.W. Tozer gives an example of what it means to dedicate yourself totally to the Lord as a sacrifice of prayerful worship. He says, "Do you know what mental prayer is? I mean: do you know what it is to pray continually? Brother Lawrence, who wrote *The Practice of the Presence of God* said, 'If I'm washing dishes I do it to the glory of God, and if I pick up a straw from the ground, I do it to the glory of God. I'm in communion with God all the time.' He said, 'The Rule tells me that I have to take time off to go alone to pray, and I do, but such times do not differ any from my regular communion.' He had learned the act of continuous and unbroken fellowship with God. So should it be with all of us."

The second concept that can help us to "pray constantly" is the idea of dedicating the day to the Lord by stopping at brief regular intervals to pray. This practice is described in both the Old and New Testaments. The Old Testament speaks of praying once a day (Ps 5:3), twice a day (Ps 88:1), three times a day (Ps 55:17; Dn 6:10), and seven times a day (Ps 119:164). The New Testament mentions that the apostles were sometimes praying around noon (Acts 10:9), in the afternoon (Acts 3:1), and at midnight (Acts 16:25). Throughout the history of Christianity, men and women have taken time during their day's activities to pray. For us, too, such a practice can help us to be aware of God's presence throughout the day.

For the last two years, I have adopted the simple routine of stopping to pray at five set times of the day: upon rising, after breakfast, lunchtime, suppertime, and at bedtime. Since these are natural breaks in my day, I found that it took only a few weeks to train myself to stop for a moment of prayer.

Five times a day, then, I simply take a moment to place myself in God's presence by praying the Lord's Prayer, and then I pray briefly for the particular theme I have associated with that time of the day. At the first prayer time I pray for leaders of the Christian churches, especially those who lead my own denomination. After breakfast, I thank God for giving me the scriptures and dedicate myself again to studying and obeying his word. Often I will read one of the eight-verse stanzas of Psalm 119 or else meditate on a single verse like verse 97 which says, "Oh, how I love thy law! It is my meditation all the day." At lunchtime, I pray for the needs that have come up during the day, using that moment to remind myself to rely on God as I continue my labors for the rest of the day. Psalm 68:19 has helped me in this respect, and I usually make it my own prayer during this lunchtime hour, "Blessed be the Lord, who daily bears us up; God is our salvation."

Before dinner, I pray for all those who need to hear and accept the saving gospel of Jesus Christ, especially those who will die in the coming night. And finally, I end the day as I began it, praying the Lord's Prayer once again and spending a moment reviewing the day and repenting for any ways in which I failed God during it.

In summary, it can help to set aside specific

times of the day for a brief moment of prayer. The Lord's Prayer and other traditional prayers can help you to quickly focus your attention on God. These can be followed by a moment of free prayer, or a brief recitation of appropriate scripture passages chosen to reinforce the theme of that hour's prayer. Of course, this method of prayer is certainly no substitute for a longer period of daily prayer and scripture study, but it is one way of making sure that you pray on those hectic days when you are not able to take your regular prayer time. And it does help you every day in your effort to "pray without ceasing."

FIVE

Studying the Ways of God

GOD MADE US to love and serve him, and that is why we dedicate ourselves to daily prayer. Because God is holy, far beyond our imagining, and because he is the highest and most important being in the universe, it is a privilege to serve him in this way. God also made us to know him—to understand him and his ways, and to be filled with his Spirit so that we become more like him in all things. God's own Spirit works in us to teach us and form in us the mind of God. For these reasons our relationship with God must involve not only prayer, but also the study of God's ways and God's character. Two types of study will enhance our relationship with God. The first, and most important, is the regular study of scripture. The scriptures teach us about who God is, what he has done, and what he wants us to do. They provide examples of how he has related with his own people throughout the ages. The Bible contains stories, prophecies, prayers, and exhortations, all of which can help us become more like Christ.

The second kind of study is concerned with the actions and teaching of God's faithful people throughout history. Christians in every age have had to face situations similar to those that confront us each day. Their lives can inspire us to remain faithful in spite of the obstacles we must overcome. This kind of study is also concerned with the creeds, proclamations, and teachings of the Christian churches, which present us with an understanding of many basic truths. It often helps to study the teachings of contemporary Christians who clearly have a gift to instruct and inspire in some particular area of Christian living.

Just as it is necessary to schedule daily prayer, it is important to plan on a regular study time every week. It usually works best for me to spend Sunday afternoon devoted to spiritual reading and the study of scripture. Consider your weekly activities and then decide on a regular time each week for this kind of study.

Appreciating Scripture

Some years ago, I read *The Hiding Place,* and it permanently affected my attitude toward scripture. The book is the true story of a Dutch woman named Corrie ten Boom who was placed in a concentration camp during World War II. She and other Christians had committed the "crime" of harboring Jews, helping them to escape from the Nazis. During her first months in prison, she had to adjust to the fearful and painful conditions she found herself in. She had to learn to trust God, who was the only one who could help her through the difficulties she faced daily. Throughout this time, she had a burning desire to read scripture in order to help strengthen her trust in God. She knew that she had to hear and think about God's word daily because she needed the reinforcement of the truth during those days, which were surrounded by so much evil and so many lies.

I was impressed by the effort she made to remember scripture. As she labored each day, she tried to recall all the scripture verses that she had ever memorized in her childhood, repeating again and again the words of any hymn that she could remember. After struggling to call to mind a forgotten verse or line of a song, she would be overcome with joy when it finally came to mind. During those long years of imprisonment, she learned to appreciate the truths of holy scripture in a way that she never had before. Because of the dilemma she faced, the words of scripture became a rare treasure, a precious commodity that nourished her during her years in the death camps.

On the very day that I finished reading *The Hiding Place*, I made a decision to make scripture a greater part of my life. I decided to memorize some important passages and to review them periodically so that I would not forget them. I decided to pray the psalms daily in the same version of the Bible so that over the years I would become familiar with their style of scriptural prayer. I also decided to learn more scriptural songs and to sing them often so that they would become very familiar to me. It has taken considerable effort to implement these decisions, and I have had to recommit myself to the effort over the years, but I have seen many good effects from my labors. My prayer has taken on a more scriptural tone, so that the petitions and praises of the psalmists come naturally to mind. As I have faced daily decisions, I have been able to recall helpful passages from scripture. And my increased knowledge of the scriptures has been an invaluable aid when it comes to teaching my children and being a help and support to other Christians. But even more than all these things, it is encouraging to know that the truths of scripture are becoming part of the fabric of my life, where they cannot be lost or taken from me.

I urge you to make the same decision I did. Value and appreciate scripture as God's word, as wisdom from on high. Decide to listen attentively as you hear or read it. Decide to believe it and to store it in your mind. Decide to obey it and put it into practice in your life. If you do this, you will find that the word of God will be available to you whenever you need it, no matter where you find yourself in the days ahead.

Scripture Study

As we study the Bible we should remember that scripture is a direct and personal word from God, inspired by the Holy Spirit, as Peter says in 2 Peter 1:21. We should not study scripture the same way we might read or study another book. In most cases, we exercise a certain amount of caution when reading, testing a book to see whether it contains truth that we can accept. We reserve the right to disagree with the author. But scripture is different. The Bible is a book that tests *us* to see if *our* life contains the truth of God. And so it is important that we bring to scripture a mind open to being transformed and renewed in the will of God, into what is good and acceptable and perfect. We need to come with an attitude of submission and cooperation. For the same Holy Spirit that inspired men to write the scriptures lives within us to help us understand and appropriate those scriptures. We should begin each study time with a simple prayer, asking the Holy Spirit to inspire us and to teach us more about God's ways.

Techniques for studying scripture abound. If you do not already use a particular method, I would recommend that you begin studying the Bible in simple ways, rather than adopting complicated techniques. The simplest method consists of answering three questions:

What does it say?
What does it mean?
What should I do about it?

If you think about these questions, even taking some time to write out the answers, you will find that your time was well spent. As you delve more deeply into various scripture texts, questions will come to mind about the background of certain books of the Bible, figures of speech, symbols, parables, and idioms. At that point you might want to read some books that talk in detail about these kinds of questions. One such book is *How to Understand Your Bible,* by T. Norton Sterrett (InterVarsity Press). Both InterVarsity and Nav Press publish helpful Bible study aids. For a more detailed and orderly way to structure your Bible study, consider *The Navigator Bible Studies Handbook.* It outlines a variety of Bible study techniques, ranging from the most basic to the more thorough study techniques, and offers examples of each. Finally, a book that deals with attitudes as well as practical approaches to scripture is George Martin's *Reading Scripture as the Word of God* (Servant Books). It discusses how we must approach scripture as the word of God, spoken to us in the words of men, so that scripture can reveal God to us and form us into his people.

A technique that I have adapted for my own use involves seven specific steps. Each step is named after the first letters of the alphabet, for easy memorization. The steps are as follows:

A—Acquaint yourself: Read over the passage several times in a couple of versions.

B—Briefly summarize: Compose a one-sentence summary of the main idea.

C—Consider challenges: Note whatever challenges you in the passage.

D—Determine difficulties: List anything you

don't understand, have questions about, or need to study further.

E—Explain difficulties: List possible answers to the difficulties as you study them or think about them.

F—Follow up: Write down one simple, specific action you will take to apply some part of the passage.

G—Give thanks: Thank God for teaching you through this study.

This method is very flexible. At times I spend only a few minutes on each item, while at other times I devote a good deal of attention to particular elements. The method can be used for individual study or as an outline for group discussion. However you use it, it will help you organize your thinking. If you want, you can approach your reading more precisely by writing out the answer to each step in a special Bible study notebook. This method, or some other technique, can help you organize your Bible study so that you can accomplish more for your efforts.

The Right Equipment

To begin your Bible study, be sure to choose a readable translation of the Bible. It is best to use a fairly literal translation of the Bible as your main Bible. The Revised Standard Version, New English Version, New American Standard Bible, and New International Version are all easy to read and fairly literal Protestant translations. The New American Bible and the Jerusalem Bible are similar Roman Catholic translations. I recommend that you use one version consistently as your main Bible, rather than using several versions interchangeably. This makes memorization and familiarization with the scriptures much easier. With this basic Bible you can begin to use the simple study method of reading and thinking about various scripture passages.

It is also helpful to choose a Bible that contains cross references, notes, and a simple concordance to help you in your study. I use the Harper's Study Bible, but there are many different ones to choose from. When you select a study Bible, keep in mind that the notes all reflect the editors' attitudes and interpretations, points of view that may be distracting or even offensive to you. For this reason, it is best to borrow someone else's study Bible for a while so that you can become acquainted with it before investing in one yourself.

Next, it helps to have two more things: a notebook, and an alternate translation of the Bible. With the notebook you can organize and record the results of your studies. A three-ringed notebook will allow you to rearrange and add to your notes as you progress in your studies. The alternate translation can give you added insight into the possible meanings of the different passages you are studying, especially passages that are hard to understand in the main version you are using. I have found the Good News Bible helpful for this purpose, but other paraphrases or freer translations could be used, such as the New Testament in Modern English, translated by J.B. Phillips, or the Living Bible.

These tools can be used in three ways. The first and simplest is to record in your notebook any interesting passages you come across in your prayer time. Then in your Bible study time you can follow up on these passages, reading any given passage several times in both your study Bible and your alternate translation, comparing the two and thinking a bit about the primary meaning. The second way involves investigating these passages more thoroughly. Note the cross references listed in your study Bible for that passage, and read those parallel passages for a better understanding of the passage you are studying. Often the parallel passages will themselves have cross references which can lead you to an even deeper study. You will want to consider any footnotes in your study Bible that explain the meaning of words or the historical context of the passages being studied. You can also make a note of the main words contained in the passage you are studying and then use the concordance to find other passages in which those words occur. A study I once did on the word "sabbath" led to many passages which, together, gave me a much better understanding of the concept. The third way to use these tools is to read through an entire book, such as a gospel or epistle, to study it for a fuller understanding of the message of scripture.

If you want to delve even more deeply into the meaning of scripture, several other tools will be worthwhile. One is a topical Bible, such as *Naves Topical Bible,* which is simply the Bible arranged according to subjects or topics. You can look up a particular word or concept, much as you would look up a word in a dictionary, and find all of the main scripture verses about that word written out for you, thereby making it easier and quicker to read a large number of passages. A topical Bible can give you more information than the concordance in your study Bible because it lists not only the passages that contain the exact word being studied but other passages that talk about the same concept even though they do not use the same word. You might also want to buy an exhaustive concordance, such as *Young's* or *Strong's.* The exhaustive concordance differs from the small concordance in your study Bible. It lists every scripture verse that contains the word in question. This kind of comprehensive concordance is especially helpful when you are searching for a particular Bible verse or when you want to do a very thorough study of a particular word.

Bible dictionaries and Bible commentaries are also worth considering. A Bible dictionary explains the meaning as well as the historical and cultural background of many biblical and religious terms. One advantage of the dictionary is that it lists terms like "Trinity" or "Bible," words that are common but do not themselves appear in scripture. When using a Bible dictionary, keep in mind that it usually contains a large amount of scholarly material, and this material may not be particularly helpful for the study you are doing. So you need not feel obliged to read everything that the dictionary has to say about the particular topic because it can easily distract you from your Bible study. Again, you must choose and use this tool with care. Not every Bible dictionary is reliable. Unfortunately, some are not written from a faithful Christian perspective and can even undermine your fath as you use them. I have found that the *New Bible Dictionary* by J.D. Douglas (Eerdmans Publishing Co.) is a helpful presentation from a Protestant perspective, and *Dictionary of the Bible* by John L. McKenzie (Doubleday) is a good presentation from a Catholic perspective.

A commentary or set of Bible notes can help you to undertake a more systematic Bible study. Some, like the *Jerome Bible Commentary* (Prentice Hall), comment on almost every verse in the Bible, while others, like Damasus Winzen's *Pathways in Scripture* (Servant Books), cover broad sections of scripture and offer a book-by-book guide. Some people prefer to use popularly written study guides, such as the *Bible Study Starters* by Peter and Vita Toon (Servant Books), as tools to structure their study of particular books of scripture.

Commentaries suggest possible meanings for various scripture passages. They vary in approach from skeptical to faith-filled, and are written in styles that range from conversational to highly technical. The best way to choose a good commentary is to ask for recommendations from someone you trust. Whenever possible it is best to borrow a commentary for a while before deciding to purchase it.

When you read scripture, keep in mind that it is best to begin with the sections that will be most helpful and straightforward. I have found the Gospel of Mark and the Book of Acts, in the New Testament, and First and Second Samuel, in the Old Testament, to make for fast-moving reading which can teach a lot about God's ways with his people. Since our goal is to learn more about God and his ways, it is not necessary to begin with Genesis and read the whole Bible sequentially, nor to begin with some of the more difficult or repetitious books like Revelation and Leviticus.

There are numerous ways to study scripture. Many types of books and cassette tapes can be purchased to guide you in that study. But no technique and no tool will help you learn the word of God unless you first begin to study the Bible itself, regularly and systematically, without worrying about techniques or tools. Begin this week with a Bible and a notebook, and decide to study an hour a week for one month. Find someone else who does regular scripture study and talk to them about their experience. Then establish your system for studying God's word as the Spirit leads you.

SIX

A Servant's Life

CHRISTIANS ARE to have the hearts of servants—doing all things for the love of God and his people. Jesus himself told us, "Whoever would be great among you must be your servant, and whoever would be first among you must be your slave; even as the Son of man came not to be served but to serve" (Mt 20:26).

When we think about growing closer to God, we might think primarily of improving our prayer life. But as we try to put the Lord first in our life, he invariably calls us to reach out to others. St. Paul tells us that those who are worthy of God's call should "fulfil every good resolve and work of faith by his power" (2 Thes 1:11). His advice to us is never to be "weary in well-doing" (2 Thes 3:13).

Serving others is a powerful way to grow in our own relationship with God because such service touches our most basic attitudes about ourself and our independence. Often, service can be the furnace that helps "purify us." When we serve others, we allow God to form us according to his plan. "Take away the dross from the silver, and the smith has material for a vessel" (Prv 25:4).

Why Serve?

I was raised in a good Christian home in which I was taught from an early age the value of serving my family. Throughout my childhood and early adult years, I was conscientious about helping out whenever I was needed. But as I look back at those years, I realize that my main motives for serving in this way were duty and need—somebody had to do it. In fact, whenever I heard the gospel story of Mary and Martha, I felt sorry for Martha. Hadn't she taken charge of a hectic situation and then been rebuked for her efforts? It seemed to me that Mary had picked a very poor time to just sit around appreciating Jesus! But Jesus did not see the situation that way. My reaction to this story was a constant reminder that my standard of judgment was not yet the same as his.

While duty is important and it is right to help when there is a need, I have learned that these two motives for serving are not the most important ones. Jesus summarized the whole law in two commands: Love God with all your heart and soul and mind, and love your neighbor as you love yourself. These commands show that our service should be motivated by love of God, from which then proceed motives of duty and mercy.

Love is a strong motivation for human beings. It is most evident in a mother caring for a newborn child. Out of love and tenderness she tries to meet all the needs of this new baby, no matter how demanding. Love is what motivates parents to make so many sacrifices in order to provide for their children. All our efforts are made much easier and more pleasant when they flow out of love for the person being served. This may be one reason why St. Paul tells us in Ephesians 6:5 to do all our service as if we were serving God and not men, so that when we serve a taskmaster who is hard to please, our love for God will lighten the labor.

We should serve because it is a privilege to serve God and his people, and because it pleases God, whom we love with all our heart. Jesus' life gives us the best example of service that we have. He served out of love for his Father. So we too should frequently renew our love for God, in word, attitude, and deed, and enter into our service with the conscious knowledge that we are serving the Lord.

Who Should I Serve?

Service involves more than volunteering to work for charitable organizations, working in a soup line, or manning a crisis center phone line. Organized programs offer effective ways to serve the community at large. But if service is to form a part of our relationship with God, it needs to involve more than occasional formal activities. It needs to be integrated into our daily lives, in both formal and informal ways. We need to take on the attitude of a servant in every aspect of our lives.

In fact, before we can serve others with the

proper attitude, we need first of all to be serving God by the way we live. As has been pointed out before, daily prayer and regular scripture study are ways of serving the Lord, offering him the praise and worship he deserves as the Creator of all things. Likewise, we can perform other activities, such as fasting or tithing out of a desire to give glory to God. If we begin by serving God well, we will be able to effectively serve the people around us.

All of us have countless natural opportunities to serve—having guests for dinner, shoveling snow from the neighbor's driveway, offering someone a ride, caring for children, and so forth. These opportunities come up in the course of normal daily living. We can choose to avoid them or to embrace them as means of growing in our relationship with God. Unless we allow the Holy Spirit to develop a servant's heart within us, we will find ourselves focusing more and more on our own needs, thereby avoiding opportunities to reach out to others.

My family has always celebrated Thanksgiving, Christmas, New Year's, and Easter Sunday together. We have always looked forward to sharing a big meal and spending an enjoyable time together. But once, on the day after Thanksgiving, when I was thanking the Lord for the enjoyable time we had spent, I sensed that he wanted to teach me something about how he wanted us to celebrate such times. Various Old Testament passages came to mind about inviting people to join in the feasts that God commanded the Jews to have. And then, as I was reading the Sermon on the Mount in Matthew, I came across the section in which Jesus says, "For if you love those who love you, what reward have you? Do not even the tax collectors do the same? And if you salute only your brethren, what more are you doing than others? Do not even the Gentiles do the same? You, therefore, must be perfect, as your heavenly Father is perfect" (Mt 5:46). I began to think of the parables in which Jesus compares the kingdom of heaven to a large banquet to which everyone is invited, until the hall is filled. I began to realize that God wanted us to invite people more often to share our festival meals, especially those who might otherwise spend the holiday alone. As a result we decided to invite four or five people with whom we normally didn't spend time to join our family celebrations at Thanksgiving and New Year.

As a family we have grown over the years in our ability to serve God in our daily life. I have noticed an attitude of joyful service taking root in all of us, especially the children. Once when my son Daniel was two years old, he brought my slippers to me as I sat resting after supper. His five-year-old sister, noticing him carrying the slippers and singing a song as he went, said to me, "I love Jesus in Danny's happiness." She had grasped a truth from this simple situation. Danny really did love me, and because of that love he spontaneously looked for ways to serve me. He received joy himself because of that service, and reflected something of Jesus in the way he served me.

By contrast, think back to the last time you had to be around someone who complained the whole time they did their work. Such an attitude benefits neither the person himself nor those around him. If service is to draw us closer to God, we must try to serve with a willing spirit, out of love for God, eagerly grasping opportunities to serve others and perform the tasks around us.

When Should I Serve?

How much time should you spend serving others? A reasonable-sounding answer would be to serve those around you whenever they were in real need of help, assuming you had the time and energy to give them. But the Lord seems to offer us an "unreasonable" answer to the question. In Luke 17:7-8 Jesus tells his disciples a story that shows just how much a disciple must serve, even when it means putting his own needs last. Jesus asked his disciples, "Will any one of you, who has a servant plowing or keeping sheep, say to him when he has come in from the field, 'Come at once and sit down at table?' Will he not rather say to him, 'Prepare supper for me, and gird yourself and serve me, until I eat and drink; and afterwards you shall eat and drink?' " Doesn't the poor servant, who has worked hard in the hot sun all day and returned home hungry, deserve some chance to eat and rest a bit before working still more? Not according to Jesus. He is emphasizing that the servant's job is to work in the field and to prepare a meal, and that he needs to do his job even when it makes life very uncomfortable. Jesus then continues, "So you also when you have done all that is commanded you, say, 'We are unworthy servants; we have only done what was our duty.'"

According to this parable our primary aim should be to do God's will, even if it means putting our own preferences and comforts aside. Having done this, we should take no special pride in our action. We are simply doing what we ought to be doing. Practically, this will mean helping people a good deal more than we would naturally be inclined to do—praying, talking, driving, giving, and in many big and small ways being available to the people around us. Sometimes we will find it easy to serve others wholeheartedly. But at other times we will find this business of serving extremely difficult and unpleasant.

But serve we must. If we serve, not by our strength but by the grace and help of the Holy Spirit, we will someday hear the Lord himself say, "Well done, good and faithful servant."

Many things qualify as our duty to God and to men. But one principle of special importance that Jesus underlined is that we are to serve one another's needs, even when it involves lowly and humble service. This was a point that Jesus stressed just prior to his crucifixion. In John 13 we are told that one of Jesus' last acts for his disciples was to pour water into a basin and wash their feet, wiping them with the towel with which he was girded. Foot-washing was normally the responsibility of the door servant, a lowly task and certainly never something that the Lord and Master would do himself. And yet Jesus did it out of love for his disciples, in order to teach them something about their position. He told them:

> You call me Teacher and Lord; and you are right, for so I am. If I then, your Lord and Teacher, have washed your feet, you also ought to wash one another's feet. For I have given you an example, that you also should do as I have done to you. Truly, truly, I say to you, a servant is not greater than his master; nor is he who is sent greater than he who sent him. If you know these things, blessed are you if you do them.
> (Jn 13:12-17)

Once we accept the fact that the Lord wants us to be humble and willing servants, there still remain many practical questions of priorities, scheduling, and the need for counsel to protect us from serving so much that we neglect own personal responsibilities. We need to learn to set our priorities wisely and to arrange our service in such a way that it is balanced by all the other necessary activities of our life. Such balance is best achieved when someone else takes a concern for protecting our life. This saves us from becoming overly protective of our time.

Individualism is highly valued in our society, so much so that we are counselled to watch out for our own interests. But the scriptural ideal calls for *unconditional* love and service, at the same time that it provides for parents, spouses, pastors, and counsellors to watch out for our wellbeing. In Galatians, Paul tells us to bear one another's burdens and so fulfill the law of Christ (6:2), and yet he also tells us that each man will have to bear his own load (6:5). Paul isn't contradicting himself. One way to understand these passages is to to say that they tell us that each of us must fulfill our responsibilities, caring for those around us, watching out for and protecting those who are under our care, all the while being able to depend on others to help us plan and carry out these tasks.

Once you have decided to serve generously, allowing the Spirit to show you how to serve those around you daily, you must also look for someone who can help you do this in the right way. Clearly, parents perform this role for their children, teaching them as they grow how to serve in wisdom. Husbands are also instructed in scripture to help their wives to do the most they can without overextending themselves. My wife and I know a couple that operate very well in this way. She is an extremely generous woman who can always be counted on to help out. Yet she and her husband discuss her schedule regularly, sometimes deciding together that she cannot help in a given situation. Her generosity is never limited by self-concern, and yet she doesn't foolishly overextend herself. Knowing the way they operate actually makes it easier for us to request help when we need it, because we realize that she will be able to say no if necessary.

If at all possible find someone to talk to when conflicts arise in your service, someone who serves the Lord generously in their own life. Make out a list of your responsibilities and a rough schedule of your week, and then talk over the situation with that person. Ideally, you should consult someone who knows you and is familiar with the way you live your life. If you cannot find this kind of help, it is still useful to make a list of priorities and to draw up a schedule, noting time conflicts or requests for service that you are not sure you can meet. Take some time to think over these requests within the context of your priorities and schedule before making your final decision. Remember that it is not automatically right to say yes nor automatically right to say no. What is most important is your basic decision to dedicate your time to the Lord and to develop an attitude of generous service. The Lord does not hold you responsible for everything that needs to be done, but he does expect you to be faithful in the things that he has given you.

SEVEN

Fellowship: An Indispensable Ingredient of the Christian Life

JESUS CAME to establish a kingdom, not a set of individual, private relationships. Ultimately, our lives as Christians must be lived in concert with other servants of Christ. The Old Testament is the history of how God called and formed a people. Even passages that focus on individuals focus on them within the context of God's relationship with the whole people. The New Testament opens with the genealogy of Jesus Christ, tying him with the people of the Old Testament, back to Abraham, Isaac, and Jacob. Throughout the New Testament Christ's followers are described as a holy race, a chosen nation, and God's own people. Revelation, the last book of the New Testament closes with a description of the New Jerusalem, in which all believers are to gather, corporately worshipping God, who is seated on the throne, and the Lamb, who is at his side. From the beginning, God intended to gather to himself a people with a corporate identity, a people who experience fellowship together. It is part of his intention that we, too, share our Christian lives together as a way of fulfilling his plan. By doing that, we gain an opportunity for growth and a source of protection.

The Need for Fellowship

Two years ago, a friend of mine decided to move across town in order to live near some other Christians he knew. He had been a committed Christian for several years, but he and his family had lived a life fairly isolated from other Christians. After struggling by themselves for a while, they felt that God wanted them to move so that they could be in more daily contact with other Christians. Once he was settled in his new house, he and his wife made it a center of hospitality, praying regularly with others, and joining with others to study scripture and share about their Christian lives. He generously gave up some of his time to serve individuals as well as his church group. And his wife and children benefited from daily contact with the Christian families in the neighborhood. The result has been major growth for his whole family. Of course, most of us won't have to move across town in order to increase our contact with other Christians, but we do need to have the same desire for fellowship. We need to be willing to pursue relationships and rearrange our schedules and priorities to insure that we live our lives in contact with other Christians.

As in so many areas of life, things go better when people join with others in their endeavors.

But more than that, the Christian life is designed to be lived out most powerfully when lived in union with others. As Jesus himself promised, "Where two or three are gathered in my name, there am I in the midst of them" (Mt 18:20). It is God's plan that his people serve him together, and he has promised to be present not only to the individual, but in a special way to his people when they gather together. It is both a natural and a spiritual principle that growth occurs more easily if a person is in contact with other people rather than alone. So we should consider ways to spend time with other Christians, taking advantage of the opportunities that are available to us.

Guidance and protection are two benefits that can come from living our Christian lives with others. Proverbs 15:22 says, "Without counsel plans go wrong, but with many advisors they succeed." As we grow in our love for God and our desire to serve and obey him, certain plans and ideas will come to mind that we think the Lord might want us to undertake. Often these can be a great source of struggle for us, either because we must decide whether we are really hearing God, or else because we must struggle through certain difficulties once we have undertaken a course of action. If we are isolated from other Christians, we are cut off from the kind of sound advice and guidance we need to make a wise decision.

I recall the experience of a friend of mine that typifies this dilemma. Soon after he and his wife decided to dedicate their lives to God, they began to take troubled people into their home to share the life of their family with them. At first, everything seemed to go beautifully. The couple felt very close to God, convinced that they were obeying his call. But before long their family began to show signs of strain, and their children experienced great difficulties with the new house guests, many of whom had serious psychological problems. The couple responded by becoming even firmer in their conviction to continue despite the obstacles. They thought it the only Christian thing to do. Finally, the husband discussed the situation with a man he respected, who immediately saw the trouble the couple had gotten into. After offering them some advice, he referred them to other Christians with experience in caring for people in their homes. As a result, the couple began to live as a family again until they learned how to channel their generosity so that it did not destroy their own family. Clearly, there is real protection in sharing your life and your plans with other mature Christians.

Praying with Others

Finally, it is important for us to pray with others. A recent article about Kathryn Koob, one of the Americans held hostage for 444 days in Iran, offers a striking example of this. For over 325 days she was kept in isolation, even to the point of being blindfolded whenever she was taken out of her room. She prayed daily through that whole time, trying to recall all of the hymns and scripture passages she had ever memorized. Then, in March of 1980, another woman hostage was unexpectedly placed in her room. The article says, "Together they studied scripture, prayed, and drew special strength from the promise in Matthew's Gospel, 'Where two or three are gathered together in my name, there am I in the midst of them.' They kept reminding the Lord that they were two" (*New Covenant,* December 1981, p. 16). Kathryn had depended on prayer during her long period of isolation, and it is easy to imagine what a dramatic difference it made to her to be able to pray with another Christian.

I have experienced similar excitement at being able to pray with another Christian after having prayed alone for a long time. When I was an officer in the Navy, I was assigned to a small ship on which there was no chaplain. We were out at sea for weeks at a time and had no Sunday services. None of the other crew members expressed any desire to pray together. So for weeks on end, while the ship was out at sea, I was spiritually isolated.

One day, the quartermaster told me that he thought I would be interested to know that a new man named Fred was being transferred to our ship. Fred had a reputation of being a Christian. I was surprised at how excited I was to hear the news. After all those months, I would have someone to pray with, to read scripture with, and to share about the Lord with! Many people were transferred to and from our ship during the years I was aboard, but none of them affected me like this one did. Waiting for Fred to arrive was like waiting for Christmas to come. Later I learned that though his ship was on the opposite ocean from mine, Fred was informed by the same grapevine that the ship he was being transferred to also had a Christian on board who liked to pray. A month later, when the transfer was finally completed, Fred and I had a good laugh over our "transcontinental grapevine." But we were also soberly impressed that, beyond a doubt, our faith in Jesus Christ needed the presence of other Christians in order to thrive.

Situations such as these make our need to pray with others readily apparent. But in the course of normal living it is all to easy to drift away from our determination to meet with others. This almost happened to me once. I had begun to meet once a week at 6:15 in the morning to pray with some friends before going to work. At first, as I set my alarm clock the night before, my determination wavered. I wondered whether the extra sleep wouldn't do me more good than the early morning prayer. But I always set the alarm anyway, knowing that the other men would be waiting for me. And when I actually showed up the next day, I was surprised at how good it was to pray with others. I would leave that prayer session reminding myself that it is well worth getting up at such an early hour to pray with others.

Paul warned the early Christians, saying, "Let

us consider how to stir one another up to love and good works, not neglecting to meet together, as is the habit of some, but encouraging one another, and all the more as you see the Day drawing near" (Heb 10:24). Although it is important to pray alone, we need to be sure to pray with others, whether it be with prayer partners, neighborhood groups, Bible studies, prayer meetings, or church services. If you have a chance to participate in some of these, don't miss the opportunity to do so. If you do not know how to make contact with other Christians, pray that God will show you how and that he will bring other Christians to pray with you. Ask him to provide opportunities for fellowship and to give you the confidence to take advantage of those opportunities. God delights to answer such prayers and to bring his people together. If you are unable to get together with others because of illness or lack of transportation or some such reason, know that the Father, Son, and Spirit are with you whenever you pray.

Corrie ten Boom once described what God taught her when her desire to pray with others was thwarted. "The church where I am speaking this week had organized a prayer meeting. I went to that meeting but nobody else arrived. I had to pray alone. Then I read Romans 8:27, 'The Spirit prays for those who love God,' and verse 34, 'Christ prays for us.' I understood then that there *had* been a prayer meeting, for if you are praying, the Lord is praying, and the Holy Spirit is praying, and that makes a prayer cell" (from *Not Good If Detached,* 1957, Corrie ten Boom, Christian Literature Crusade, 1957, p. 62).

How to Pray Together

Group prayer can take many different forms, ranging from shared silent prayer to formal liturgical worship. In more formal worship, the style of prayer is already determined. To join in, you simply need to become acquainted with the order of worship. But in informal groups, you need to agree among yourselves how to pray together.

Warner Hutchinson talks about the basic elements of group prayer in his essay, "How to Pray Together." In it he shares some of the wisdom that the leaders of InterVarsity have gained over the years. He says:

> Group prayer should include: (1) Worship—giving honor to God. This is a hard concept for us raised in a society where everyone is regarded as our equal. (2) Thanksgiving—being grateful for what God has done for us and in us. (3) Confession—acknowledging with genuine sorrow where we have failed or disobeyed what we know to be the will of God for us. (4) Petition—laying down our own needs before God. These will be needs of character and of a very practical nature. (5) Intercession—laying the needs of others before God. These will include other students, faculty members,

family, God's servants around the world, and special activities you may be planning.

He goes on to suggest that the group agree on a time and place in which to pray, as well as the duration of the prayer meeting, which he recommends last for twenty or thirty minutes. One person should be responsible for starting and ending the meeting and for giving basic structure to it. It usually works best for this leader to take the responsibility for several weeks in a row, rather than having a different leader each week. Practical details such as which songs or hymns to sing and whether to sit or to stand in a circle all affect the group's prayer (from *Essays on Prayer,* Inter-Varsity Press, 1968).

This format for prayer can work very well if the people in the group feel comfortable with it. The men I pray with weekly use a format similar to the one described. One of the men plays guitar and leads us in familiar songs, scattered throughout our half-hour prayer time. We usually take ten or fifteen minutes at the start in which to openly praise God for his goodness, speaking out short prayers or reading verses from the scripture that give glory to God. Usually we close our time of prayer with petitions for our needs and the needs of our families.

There are, of course, other ways to pray together. Once I was part of a Bible study in which the participants used the last half of the study to thank God in prayer for the things learned during the study itself. Many of the passages we studied were very inspiring, and the discussion and sharing moved us into the presence of the Lord. We found it very easy to worship God, praising and thanking him for the mystery of his plan of salvation.

Common prayer should constitute an important part of our spiritual life. We should desire it, search for it, and participate in it faithfully.

Being Together

It is important for Christians to pray and study scripture together because the basis of our relationships must be common submission to Jesus Christ. People who share a common vision about the most important truths that govern life share a very tangible strength as a result. But it is also important that Christians share good basic human relationships. In fact, this kind of basic fellowship is such a strong need that isolation can sometimes drive the non-Christian to a crisis that ends in faith. One very interesting example of this is the story of the conversion of Eldridge Cleaver. Once the candidate for the presidency of the United States on the Peace and Freedom ticket, he called himself a communist, and visited Cuba and North Vietnam while maintaining luxury apartments in Europe. He describes his life in these words:

> I found myself on a peak and then I found myself at the bottom. When I looked back at my life, trying to understand how my life turned, I

see that it was one exclusion after another. It's fantastic to see that I have gone back to being twelve years old, when I stopped listening to my mother. I couldn't stand to hear her, because she was always trying to show me a point.

Recently mom, who is sixty-nine now, said, "Up until the time you were twelve years old, you were a little angel. But when you turned twelve you turned into a little devil—the whole process of you going away and turning your back on the family and dropping out of one thing and then another."

Leaving my family, my circle of friends that I grew up with, and quitting my high school football team, eventually I was excluded from the normal and broad movement of black people in the civil rights movement, and got hung up in the very fringe element of the Black Panther Party.

There was a time when I took pride in being on the F.B.I.'s Most Wanted List, and that's the truth! But, ultimately, I was excluded from the Party and the U.S. itself! Then I found myself absolutely alone, without any idea of my self, of how to get back, of how to come out of that dead end, and how to be reunited with people and friends, not to mention coming back home!

It was only after experiencing that total isolation and exclusion that I was able to be open to receiving faith. I discovered doors opening and a process of inclusion beginnning:

the pendulum began to swing the other way! A process of reconciliation began that could not have possibly come about in any other way! I found myself, first of all, included and reconciled with my pursuers. The first step back was to be reunited with the F.B.I., who was after me, and finally to come back to the country and be reunited with family and old friends who had first scorned me with my return.

There is a process of healing taking place, and it's wonderful to be able to see how the healing power of love can build bridges between people, overcome generation gaps, racial divides, and class division. I experienced the power to break out of isolation.

I can see myself on the road to an ultimate inclusion at the end of this earthly life, when I'll be reunited with the Heavenly Father! I praise God that those things are possible and I can smile again because I have a smile inside and outside.

(Quoted from Robert H. Schuller's *The Peak to Peak Principle,* 1980, Doubleday and Company, pp. 111-113.)

As a youth, Cleaver rebelled, separating himself from the people and culture that he had been part of. He strove for fame and power, only to find that they isolated him from God and from other people. Without this basic human support, he found himself utterly alone. The words of Genesis summed up his predicament quite well: "It is not good that the man should be alone" (Gn 2:18). This realization eventually wrought a conversion in his life.

When I first became involved in a group of people that met weekly to share their Christian lives, I found that we never talked about anything but "spiritual things." Most of us were single students or newly married couples, and every week we shared about our prayer time, our scripture study, our evangelism, or our spiritual successes and failures. After a while, I found myself in the odd position of knowing a great deal about these people's spiritual lives, but very little about their jobs, families, or practical needs.

In contrast, my family and I now live in a neighborhood with several other Christian families who belong to the same Christian group that we do. Every week we meet together, sharing about our Christian lives, but also sharing the everyday aspects of life—work projects, crafts, recreation, raising children, working through illnesses, and so forth. We make a point of varying our activities so that they include time for service and recreation time as well as sharing and scripture study. This has helped draw us together in a way that gives even more meaning to the rich spiritual life that we share.

Fellowship is not an optional extra. Close relationships with other Christians provide a forum in which we can hear and apply God's word along with others who are committed to that same word. That is why Christian fellowship is so important in God's plan. Fellowship can provide an environment in which to receive both the encouragement and the redirection that we need in our Christian life—encouragement such as teaching, direction, and counsel, and redirection such as correction, reproof, and exhortation. The Holy Spirit is continuously at work to change us and make us holier, to create Christ's character in us. To draw us into deeper union with God, he helps us realize the need to turn away from wrongdoing, reorder our priorities, and apply God's word to our life. At the same time he works in us to draw us into deeper union with one another so that he will have even more ways to work in our lives.

It is obvious that it helps to have other Christans to support and encourage us when trials and difficulties arise in our lives. In such cases it is clear that the Lord uses the people around us to strengthen and support us. But it is just as true that God wants to make use of our fellow Christians when all seems to be going well in our lives.

Scripture says that Jesus Christ is to be the Lord of our lives. A lord is one who is in charge of everything. We need to merge our lives with others who have placed themselves under the same Lord. Such relationships are a sign and a reminder of our common commitment, our support in good times and bad. They become a source of protection for us and a witness to others.

EIGHT

Obstacles to Overcome

WE HAVE DISCUSSED several major ways of growing closer to God, along with various obstacles that can slow us down or stop our efforts. What follows is a list of some of the more common problems we face and suggestions about how we can overcome them. You may want to review the checklist occasionally, or you may want to use it as a springboard for discussion with other friends who have read this book. It can help to refresh your memory from time to time about the basic ingredients for growing in a relationship with God.

Obstacle	Actions
A. In the beginning	
1. Unclear goal	—Decide to dedicate your life to God under the Lordship of Jesus Christ.

2. Relying on your own effort	—Ask the Holy Spirit to empower and direct you.
3. Discouragement	—Set simple goals. Be faithful. —Expand goals as you grow.

B. Daily prayer

1. Lack of incentive	—Decide that daily prayer is necessary.
2. Lack of time	—Make a weekly schedule that includes daily prayer. —Offer your work as a sacrifice to God. —Set short times of prayer at various points in the day.
3. Inconsistency	—Pick a good time each day to pray, with a back-up time in case you miss your regular time. Make it a high priority. Set a minimum amount of time to pray each day.
4. Boredom	—Utilize different styles of prayer.

	—Study the life of an inspiring Christian.
5. Lack of growth	—Keep a notebook of prayer direction. —Increase your scripture study.
6. Prayer seems like a monologue	—Ask God questions and have periods of distinct "listening." —Keep an intercession list and thank God for answers.

C. Weekly Study

1. Inexperience	—Enter your ideas in a prayer notebook. —Use a Bible study handbook.
2. Lack of topics to study	—Enter your ideas in a prayer notebook. —Use a printed study guide. —Ask your pastor to recommend Christian biographies.
3. Inconsistency	—Schedule a weekly study time.
4. Confused results	—Discuss results with mature Christians.

—Use only one reliable commentary.
—Record inconclusive results for future study.

D. Regular Service

1. Fear of over-involvement	—Start small. —Submit your schedule to a mature Christian. —Learn to say no as well as well as yes.
2. Uncertainty of where to serve	—Begin with family, friends, and neighbors. —Schedule fixed hours for formal service.
3. Reluctance to serve	—Ask God to change your attitude. —Do a Bible study on the words *service, slaves,* and so on. —Read inspiring biographies about generous Christians. —Begin serving despite your reluctance.
4. Guilt at saying no	—Submit question to mature Christian. —Write down number of hours per week you serve.

	—For unwarranted guilt feelings, do a Bible study on grace, salvation, and so on.
E. *Regular Fellowship*	
1. No present fellowship	—Attend regular church services. —Join a small Bible study. —Search out a prayer meeting.
2. Reluctance to get involved	—Pray for a change of attitude. —Set aside time in your schedule. —Do a Bible study on people, nation, church, and related topics.
3. Too many meetings	—Decide which are most helpful and cut back to those. —Be faithful in one place instead of frequenting many.
4. Unfruitful fellowship	—Talk about it to people in charge. —Pray for the help of the Holy Spirit. —Be flexible.

Conclusion

IT HAS BEEN said that God made us in order to know him, love him, and serve him in this world and be with him forever in the world to come. In order to grow closer to God we must know who he is and how he acts. We must come to him regularly in prayer, learning to understand, appreciate, and respect him, as well as to submit to him.

God has given us his word in holy scripture, and we can use this word in our prayer, meditation, and study to help us know and understand him better. He has also given us his own Spirit, the same Spirit that raised Jesus Christ from the dead, so that we might be taught by God himself. Through our study we can come to know God and who he is. As we take that knowledge with us into prayer we can grow in a deep and steadfast love of God. We can express our gratitude, make our pleas, and give him the honor and glory he deserves. Alone and together with others we can grow to appreciate the majesty and mercy of our God.

When we know God, we are naturally led to serve him. Our life becomes a service of worship and praise; our work becomes a service of helping to fulfill God's plan and to represent him where he has placed us. When we know him, our heart goes out to the people that he loves, and leads us to serve those that he has placed around us. Service that flows out of knowledge and love of God is not motivated by a desire to earn salvation or to avoid our guilt. It is an expression of the fruit of working closely with God in our daily lives.

Finally, as we strive to communicate with God in prayer, to understand him better through study, and to find ways to serve him with others, we will appreciate the support that Christian fellowship provides. We will remember that we are not seeking God by ourselves but are moving on as a people.

One of the most important goals of our life should be to grow constantly closer to God. Consider the honor and privilege it is to be invited by the God of all creation to join him in his work. What other challenge can compare with that? What else could be more exciting or ultimately more fulfilling? It is the one goal in life that will not end with our death, but rather it will come to complete fulfillment as we enter the kingdom of God to live with him forever.

The books in the *Living as a Christian* series can be used effectively in groups. To receive a free copy of the Leader's Guide to this book and the others in the series, send a stamped, self-addressed business envelope to Servant Books, Box 8617, Ann Arbor, Michigan 48107.